I0502745

A VERY EMOJI CHRISTMAS

24 PAGE COLORING BOOK

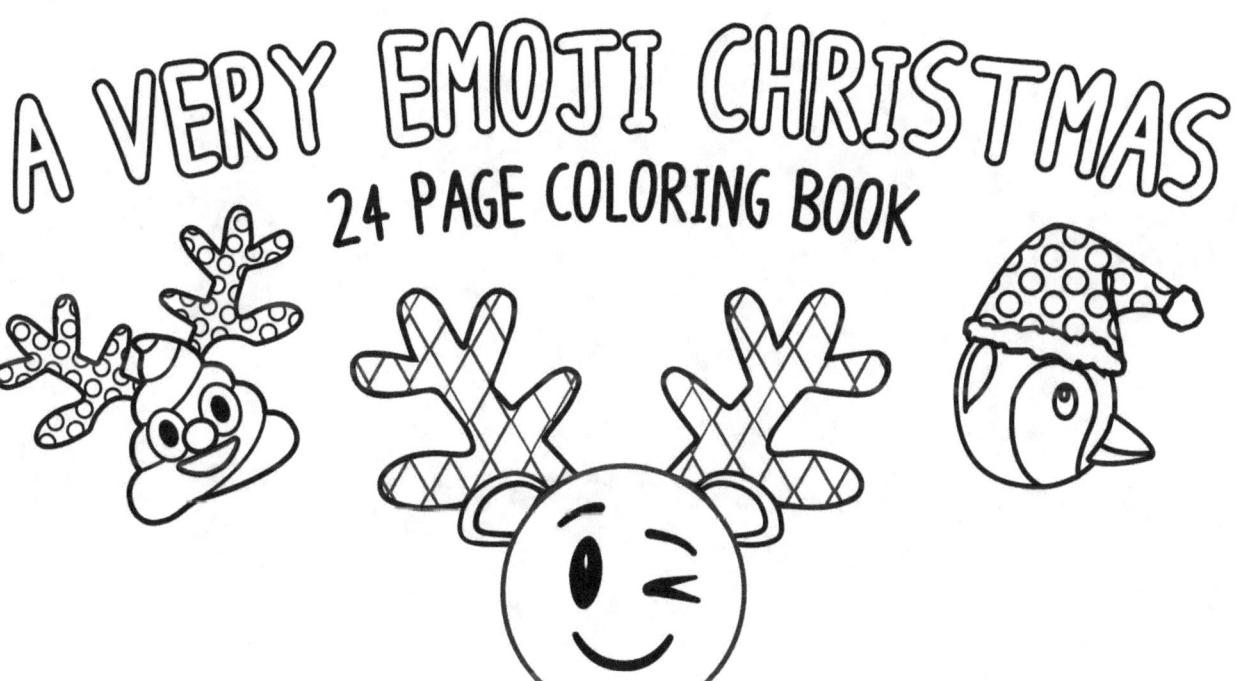

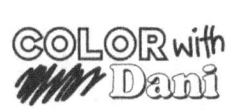
COLOR with Dani

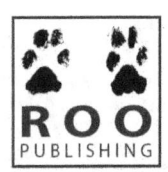
ROO
PUBLISHING

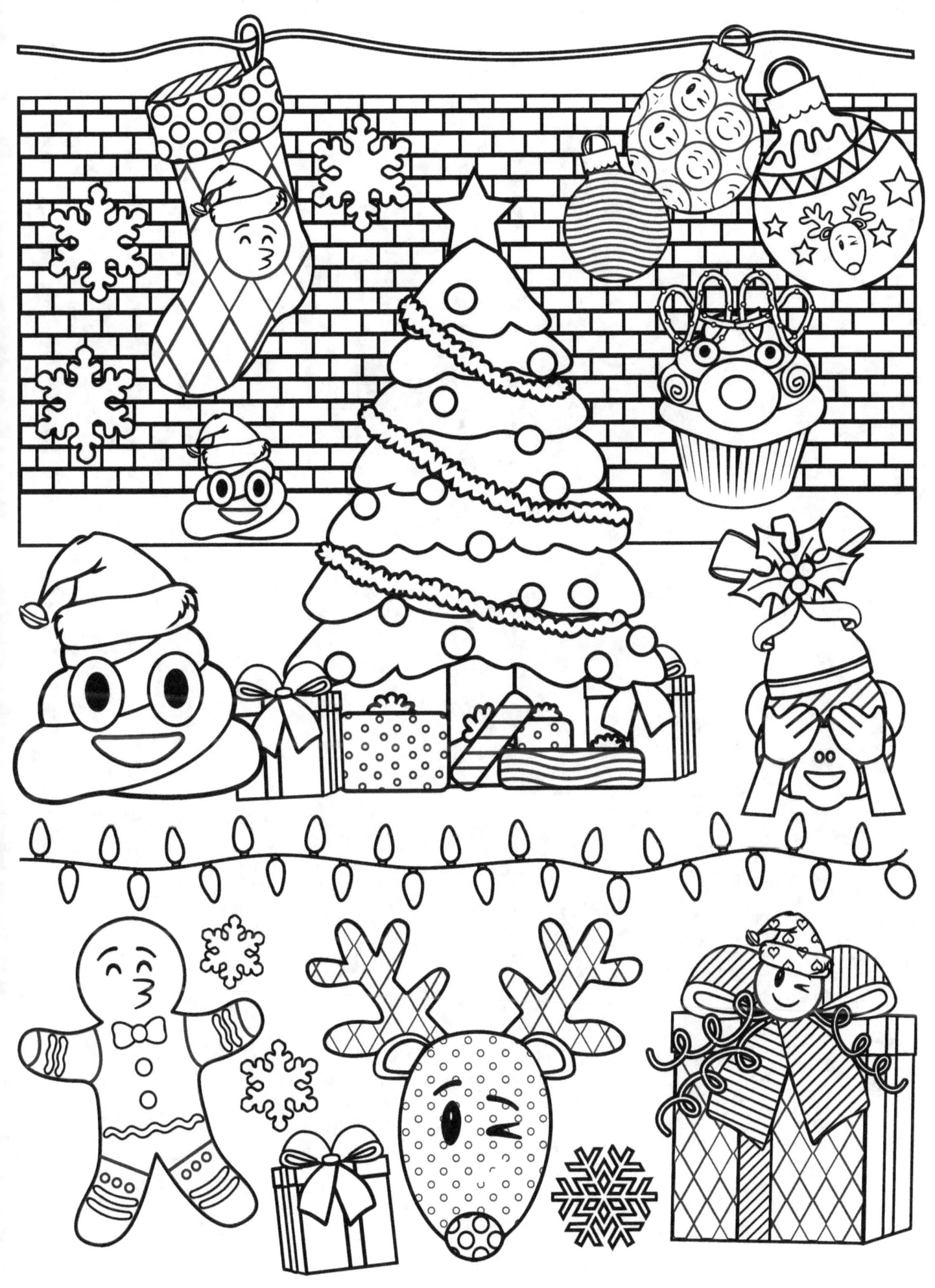

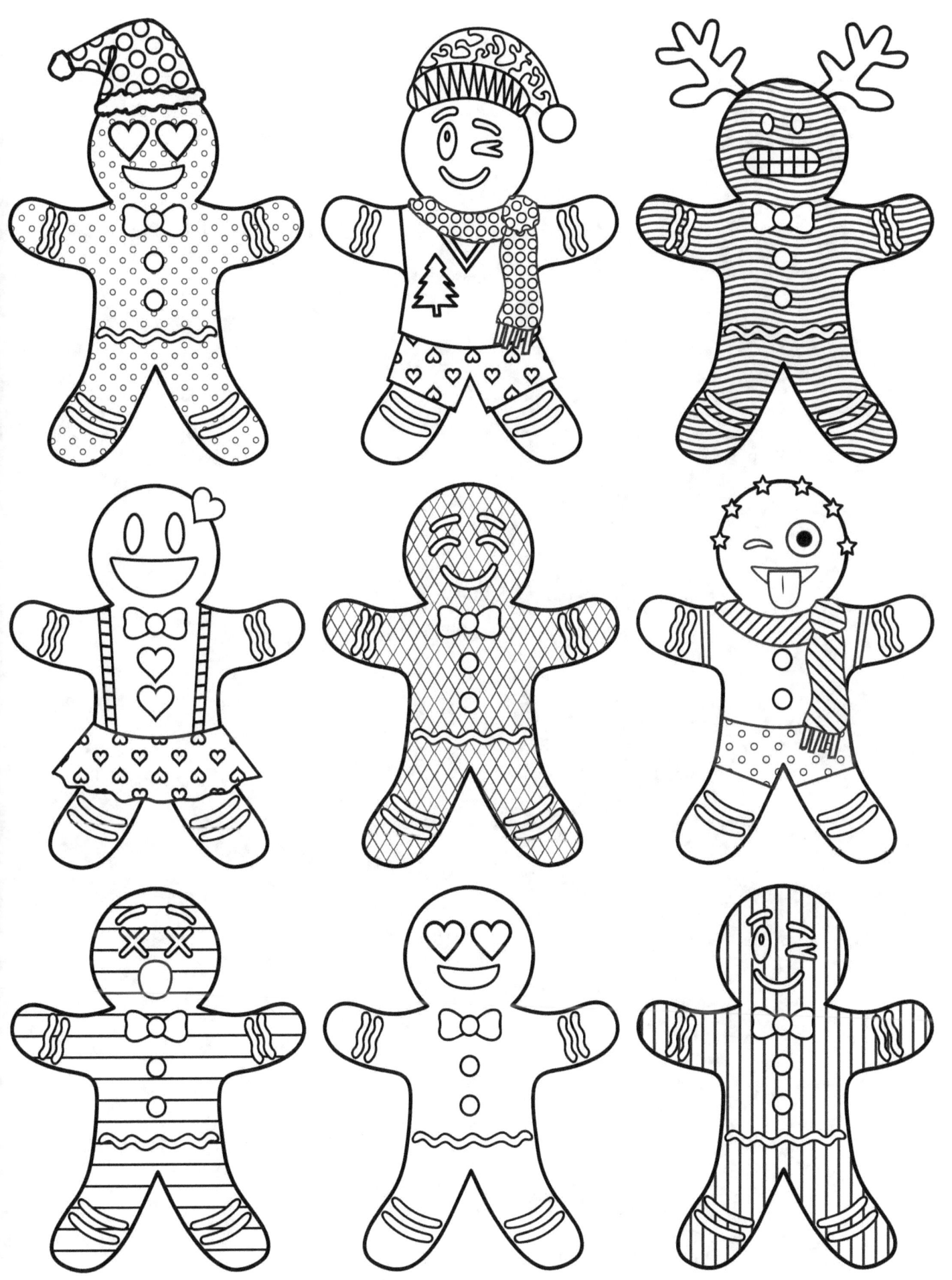

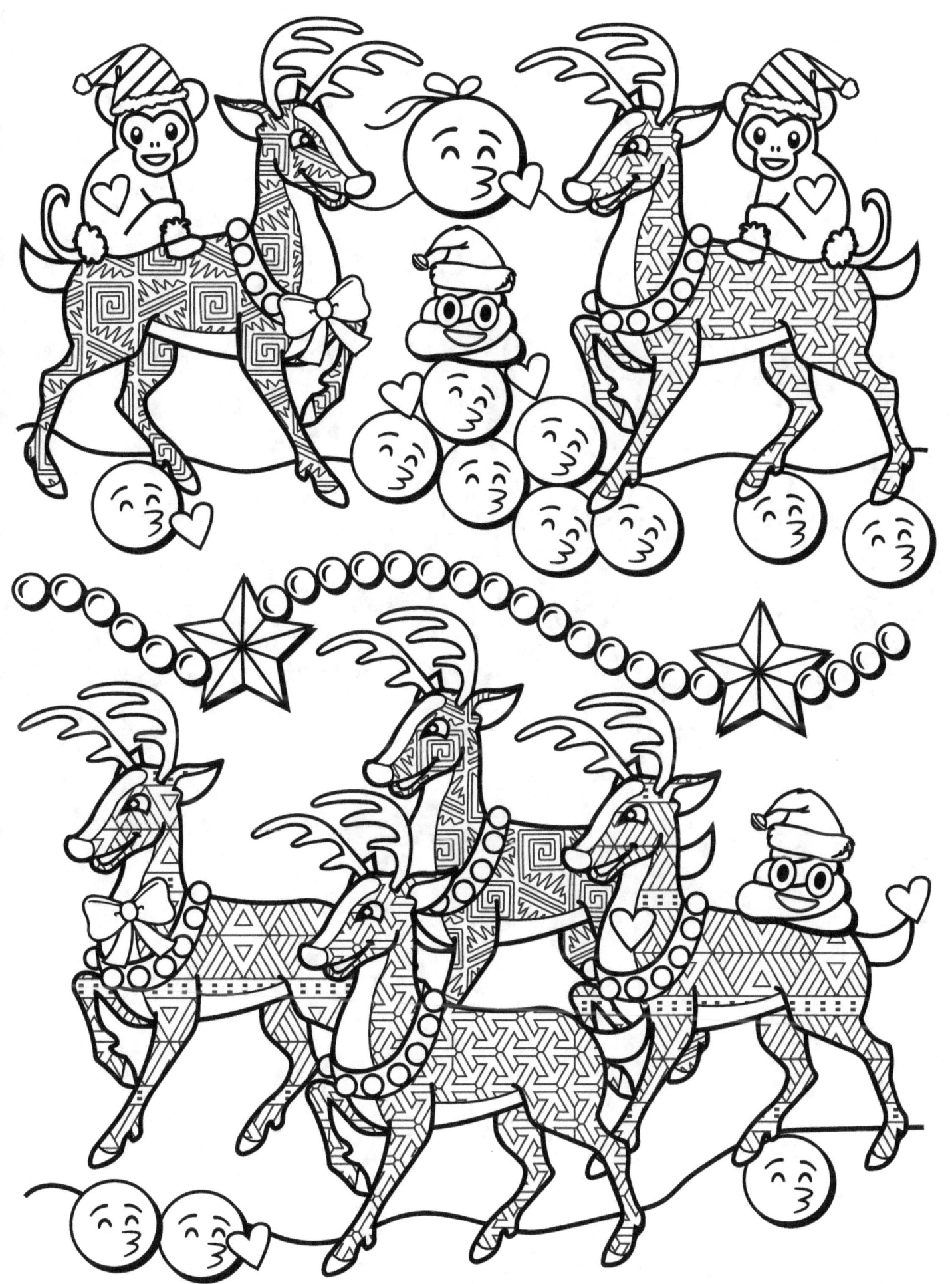

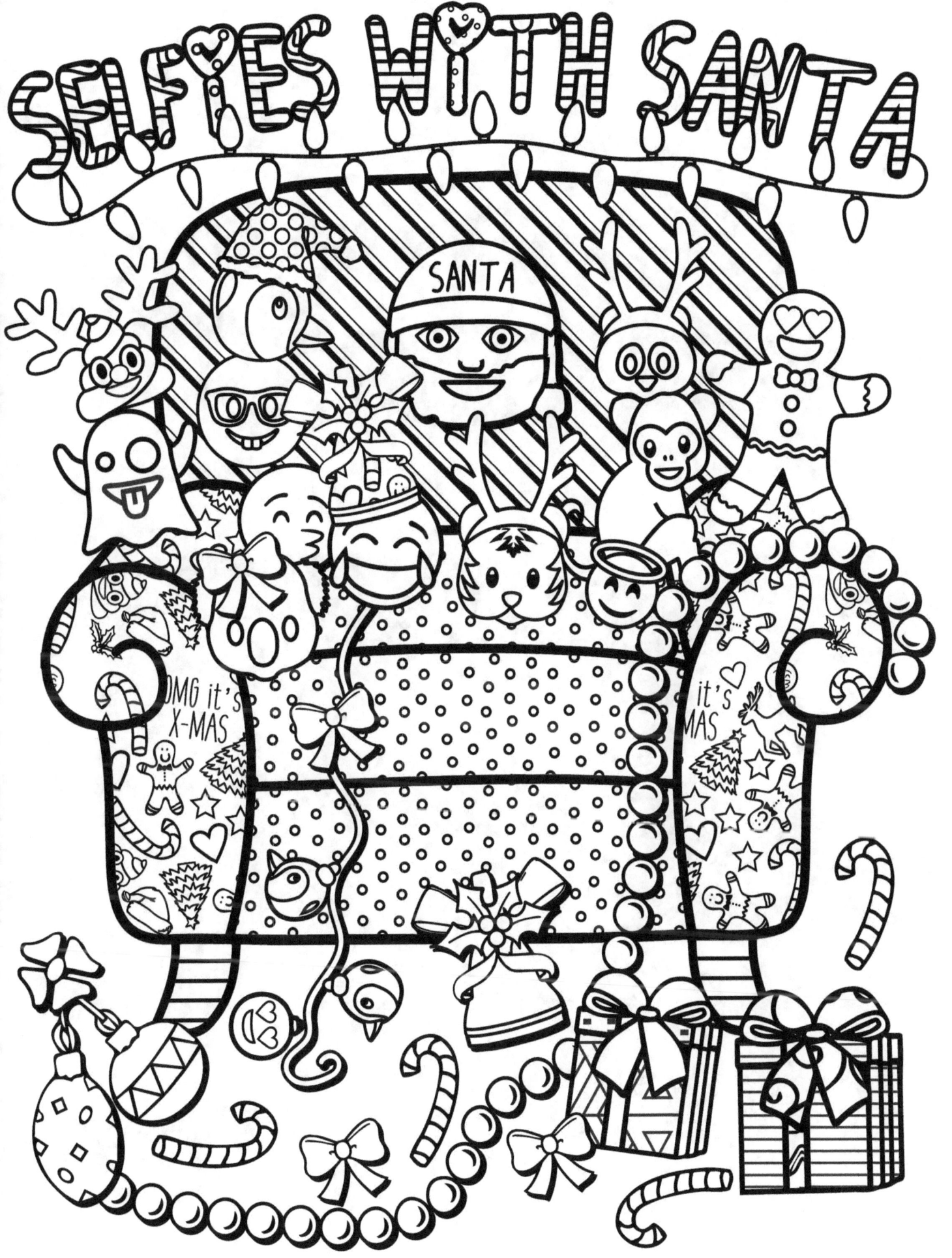

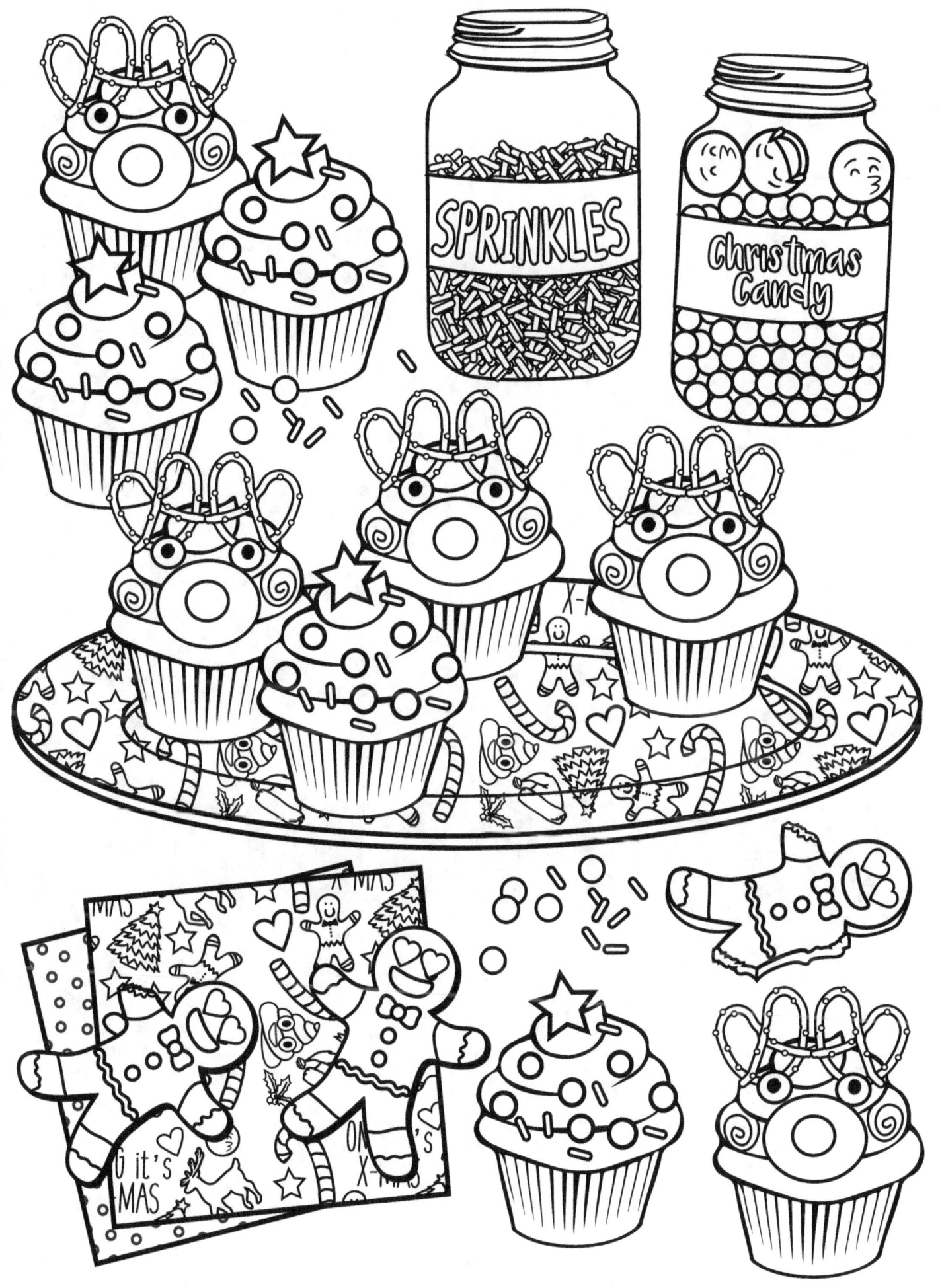

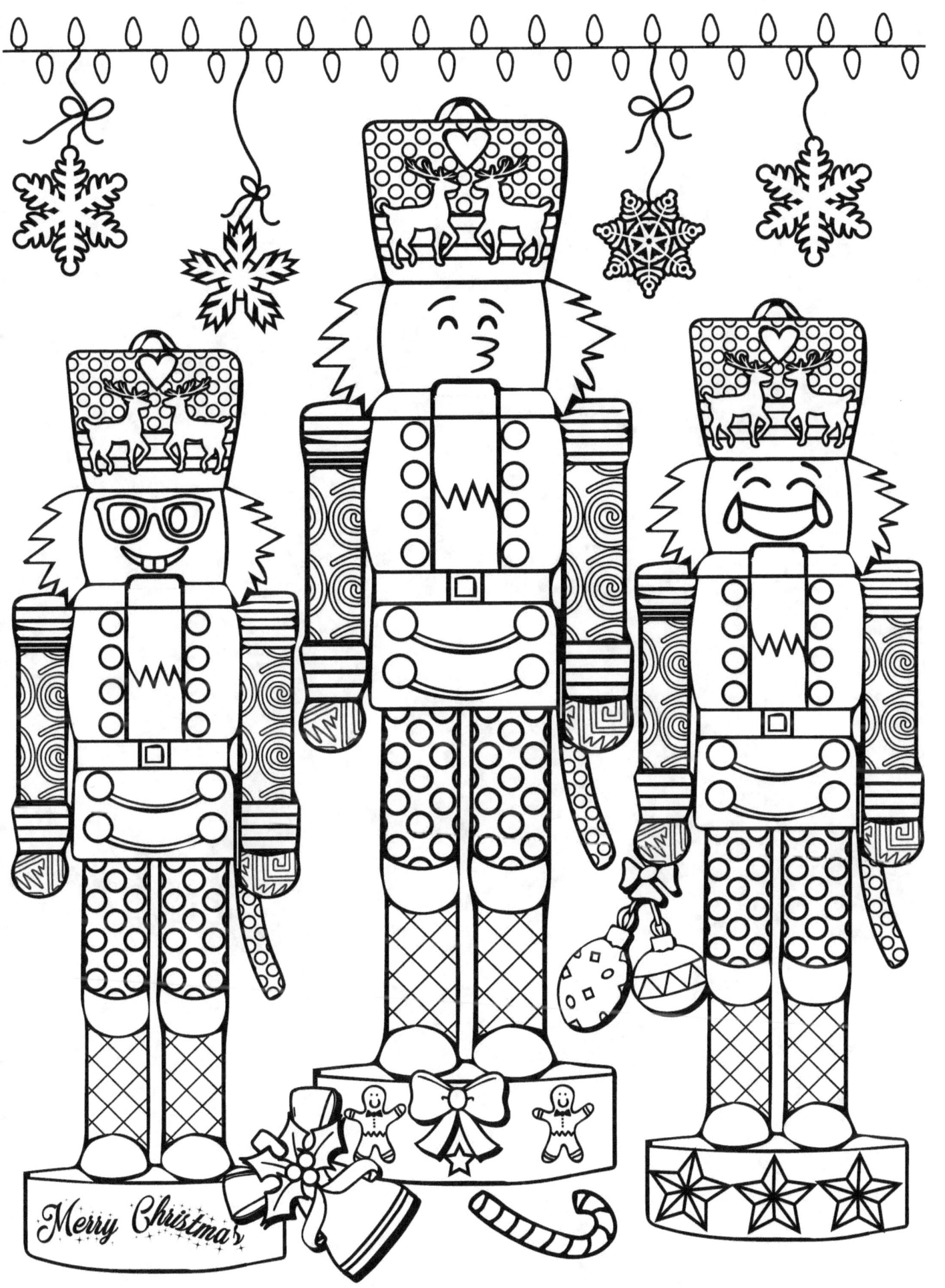

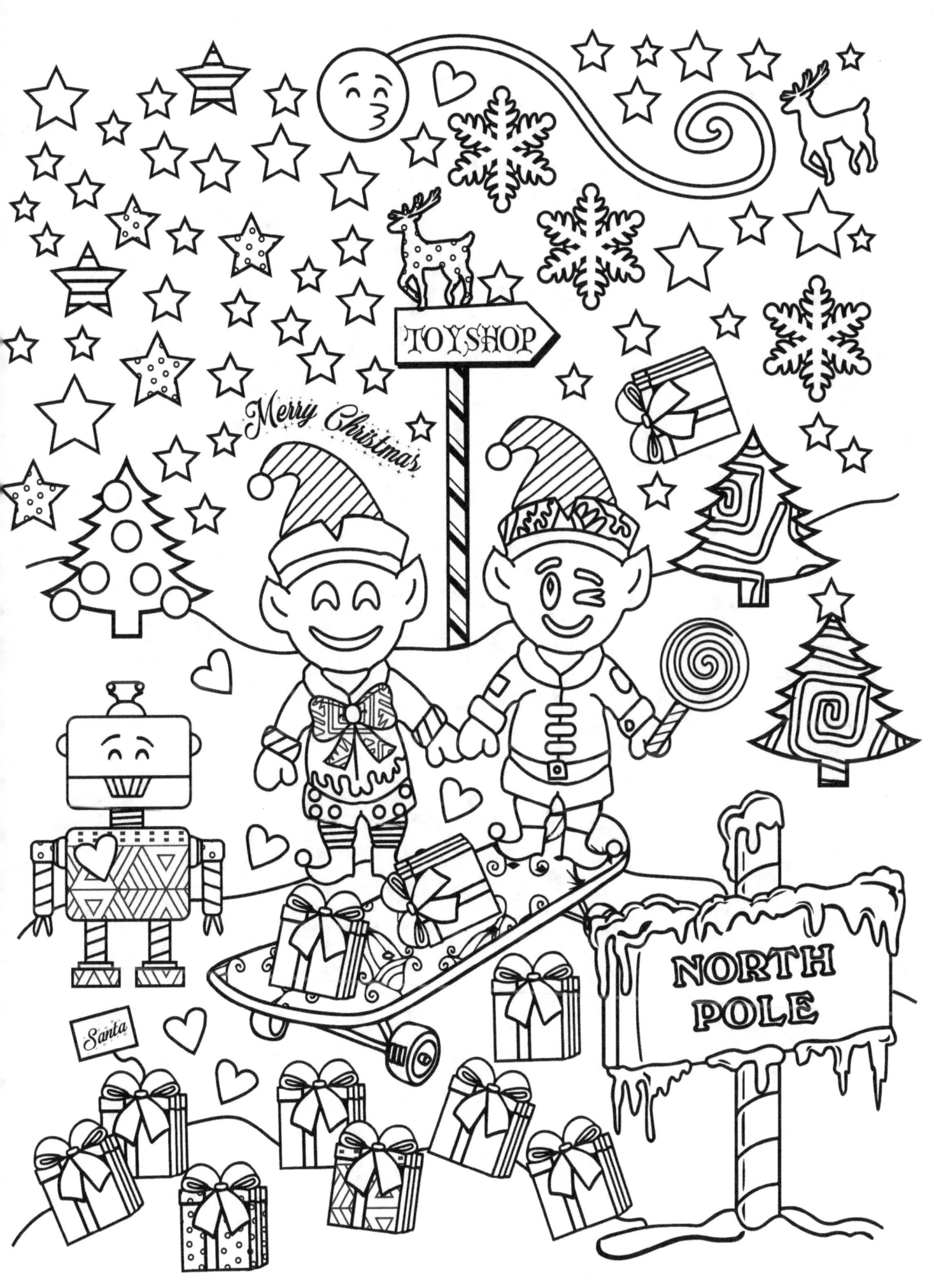

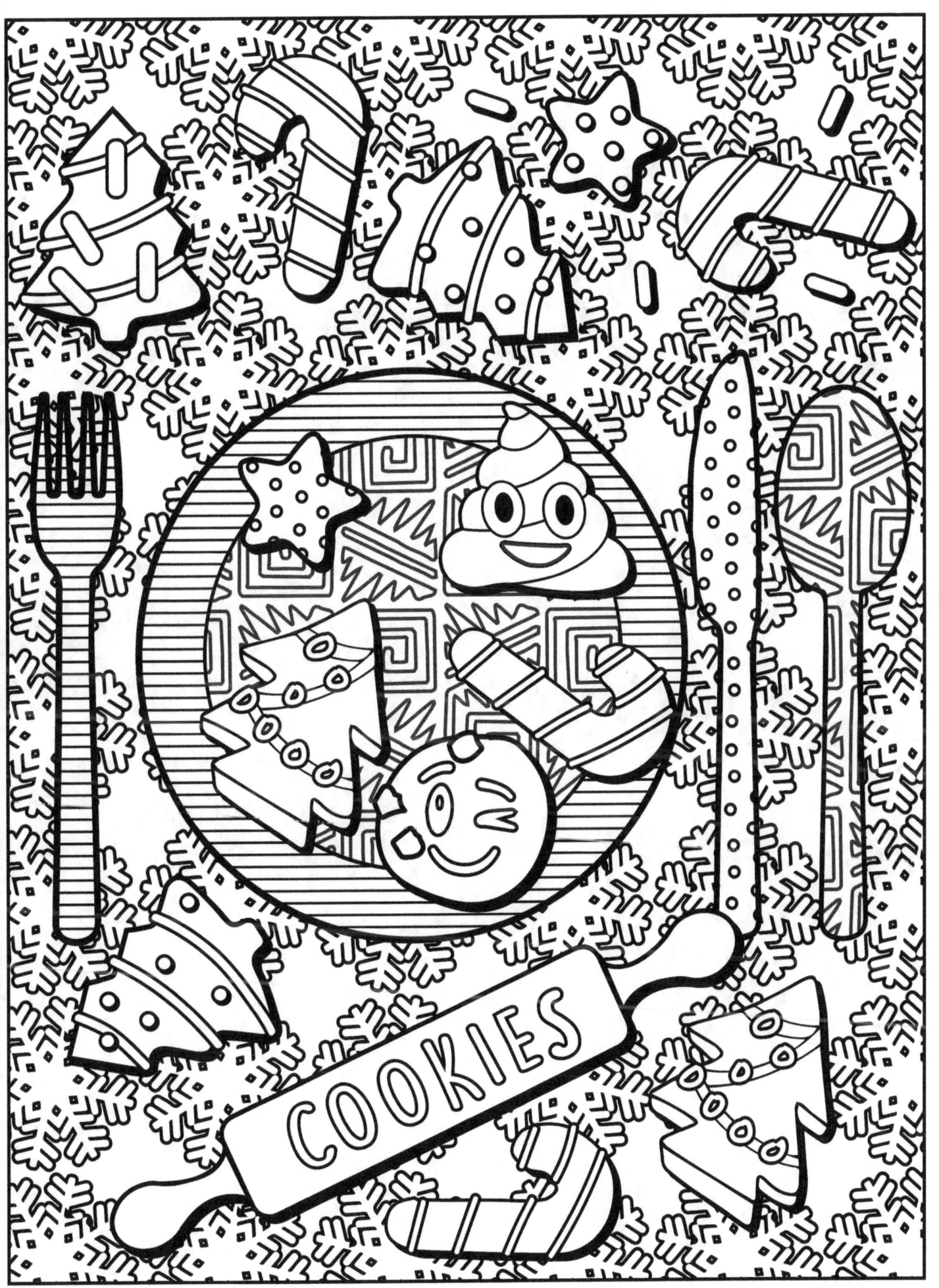

COOKIES

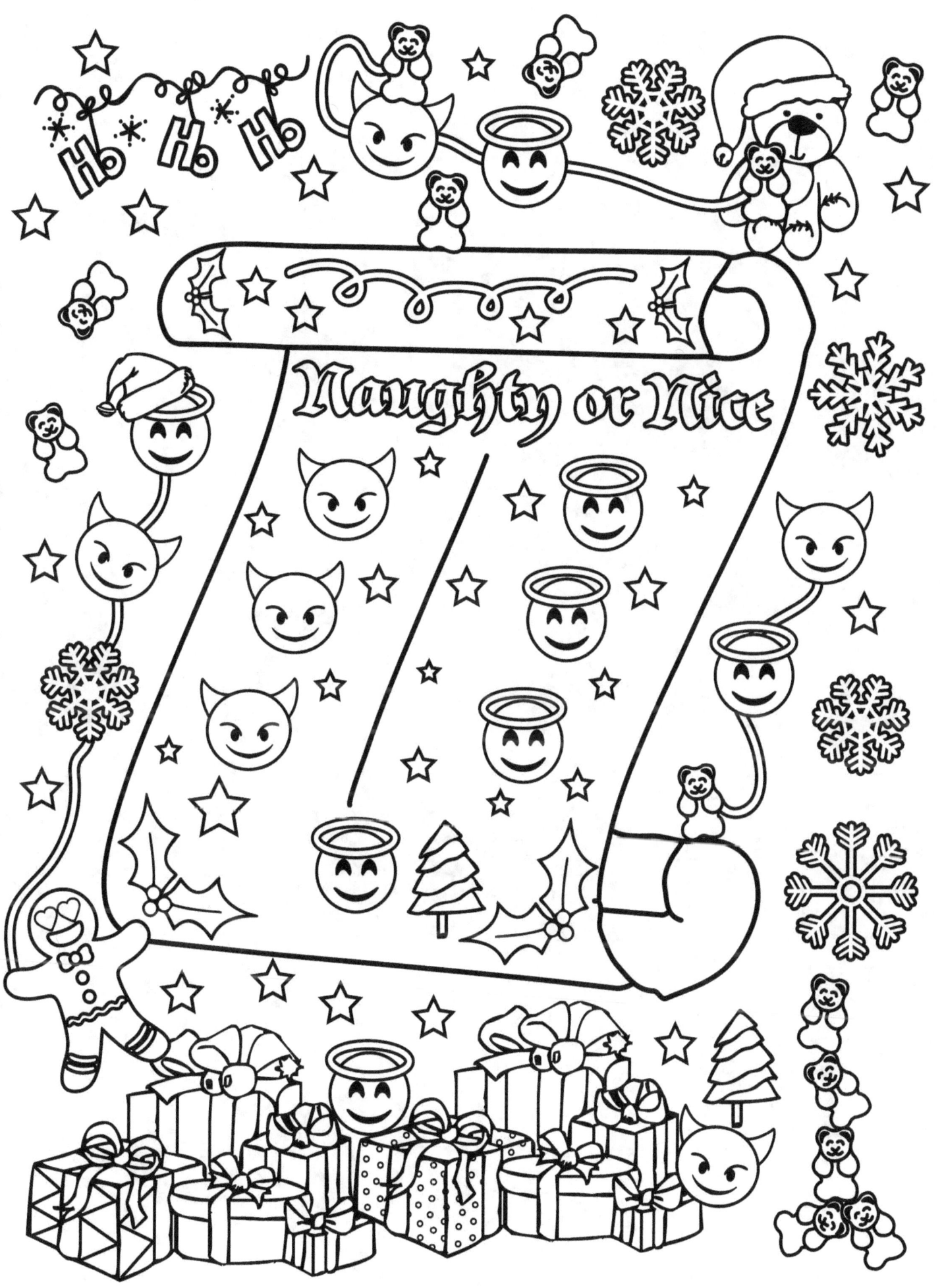

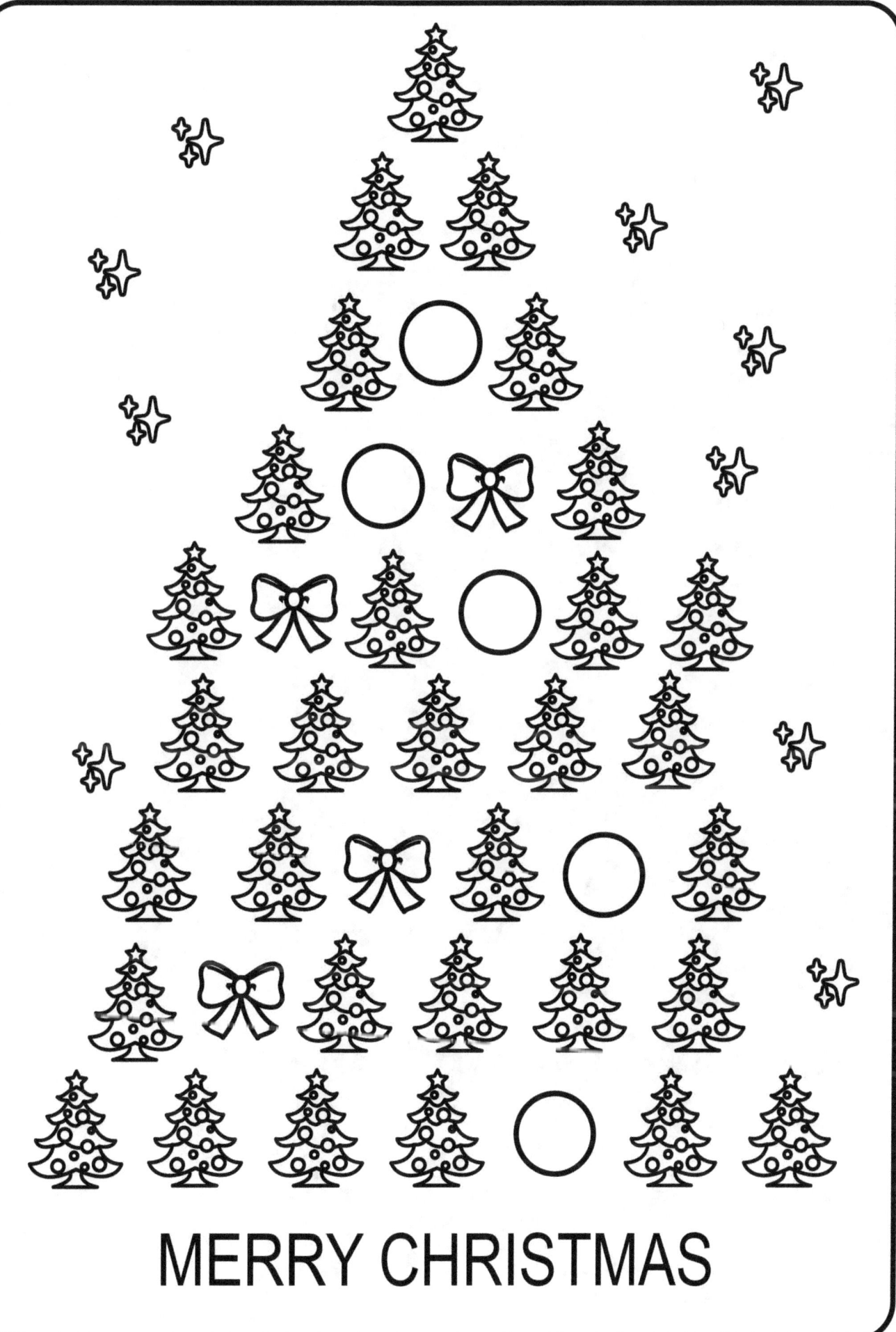

MERRY CHRISTMAS

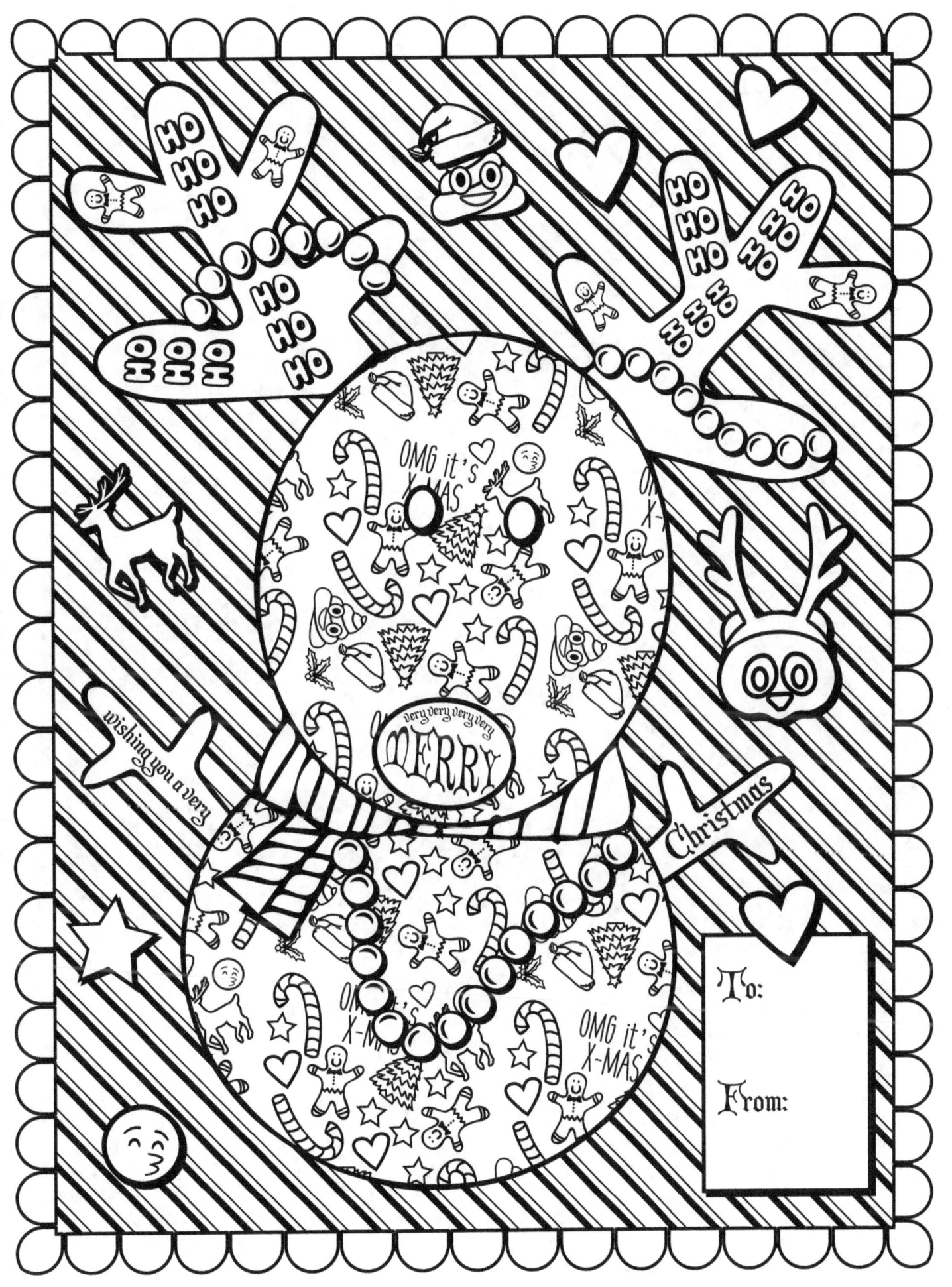

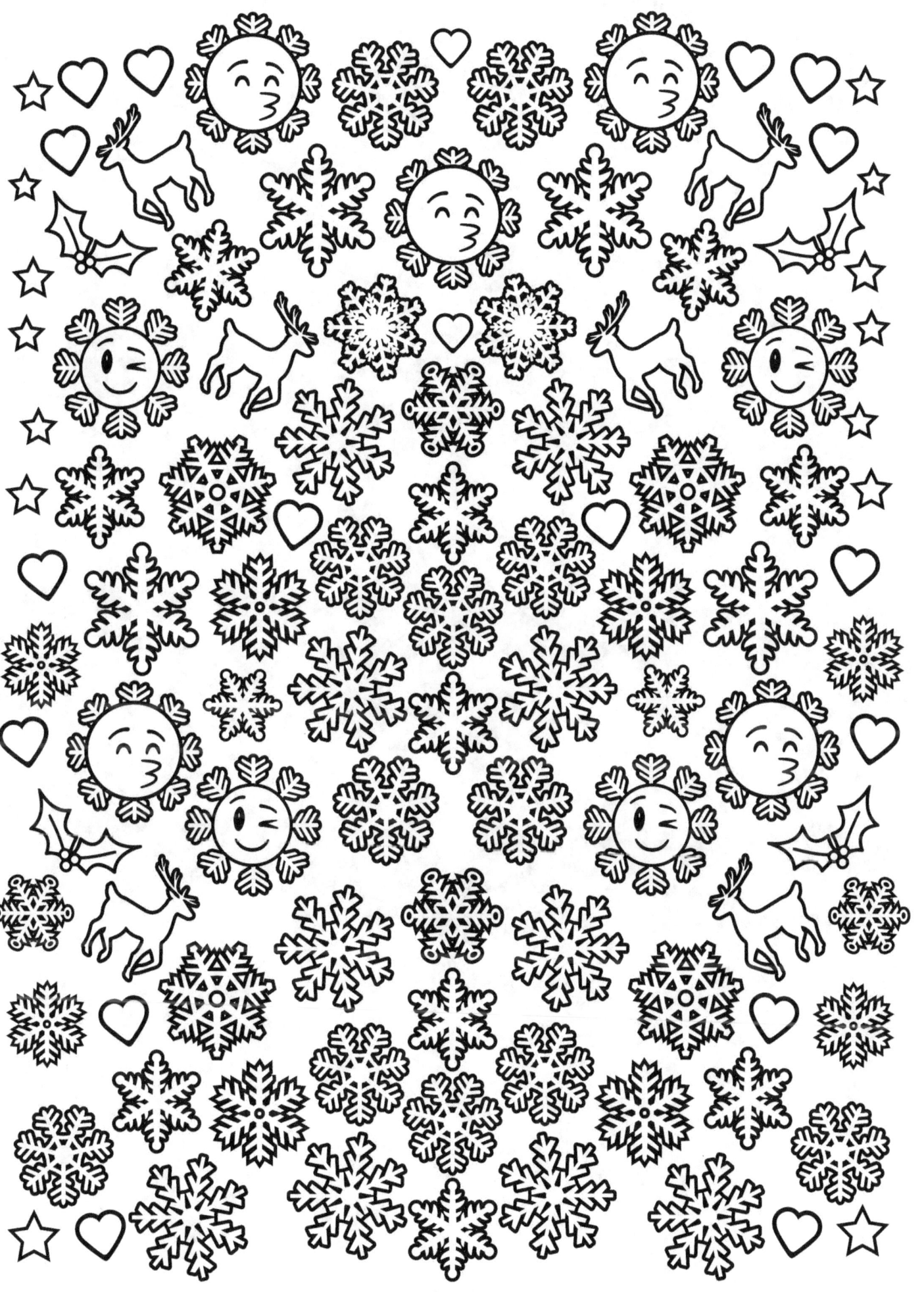

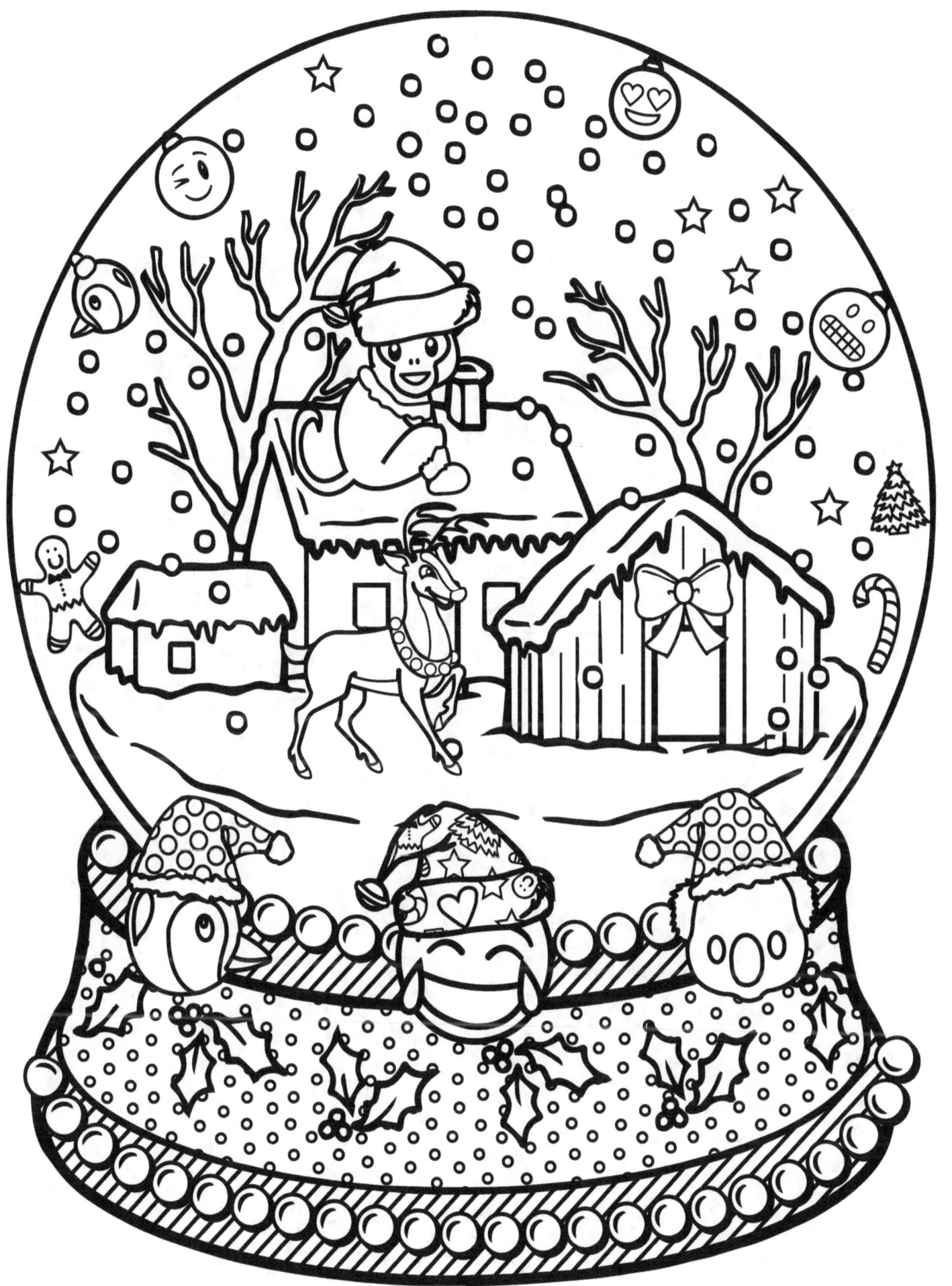

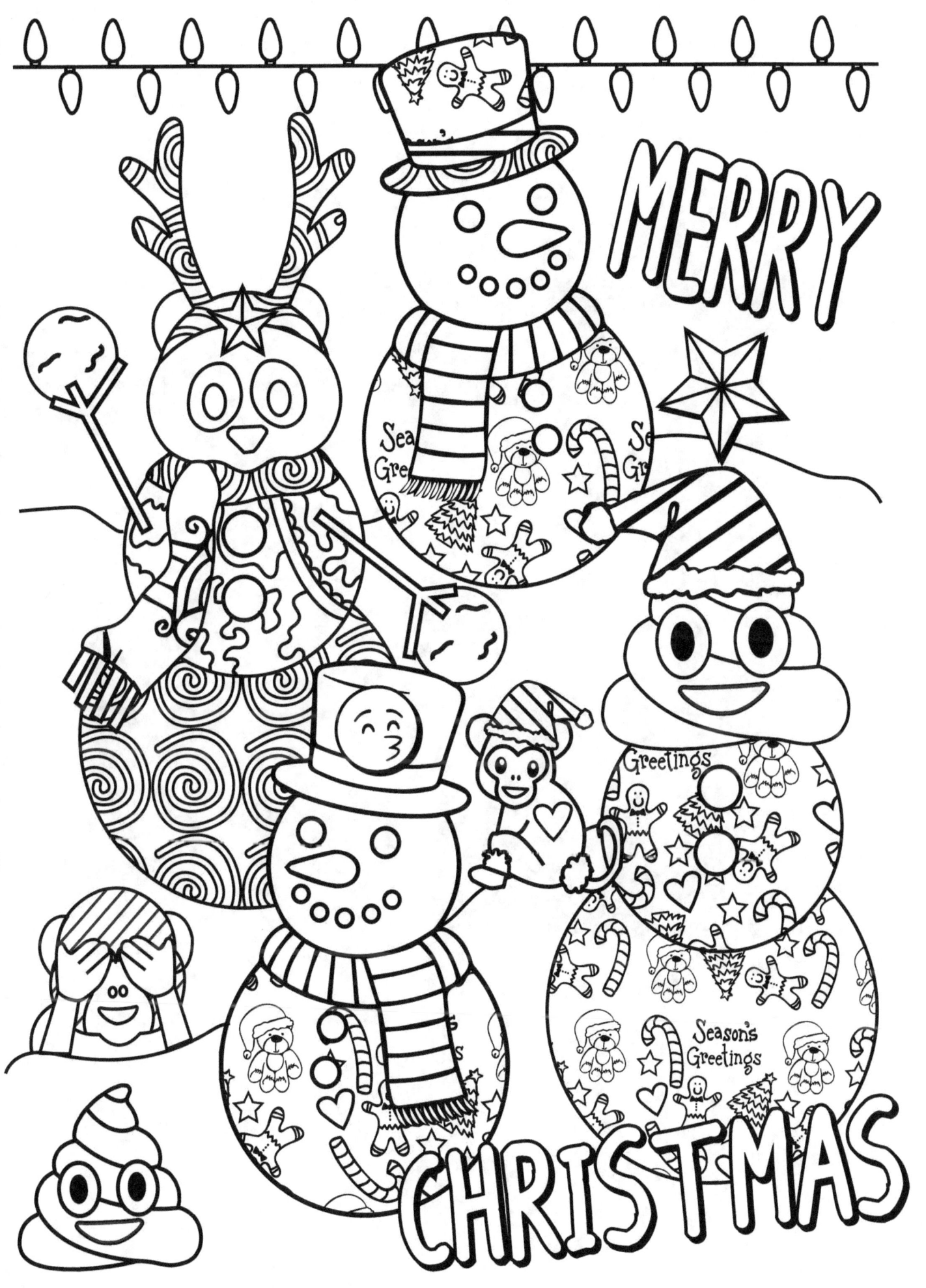

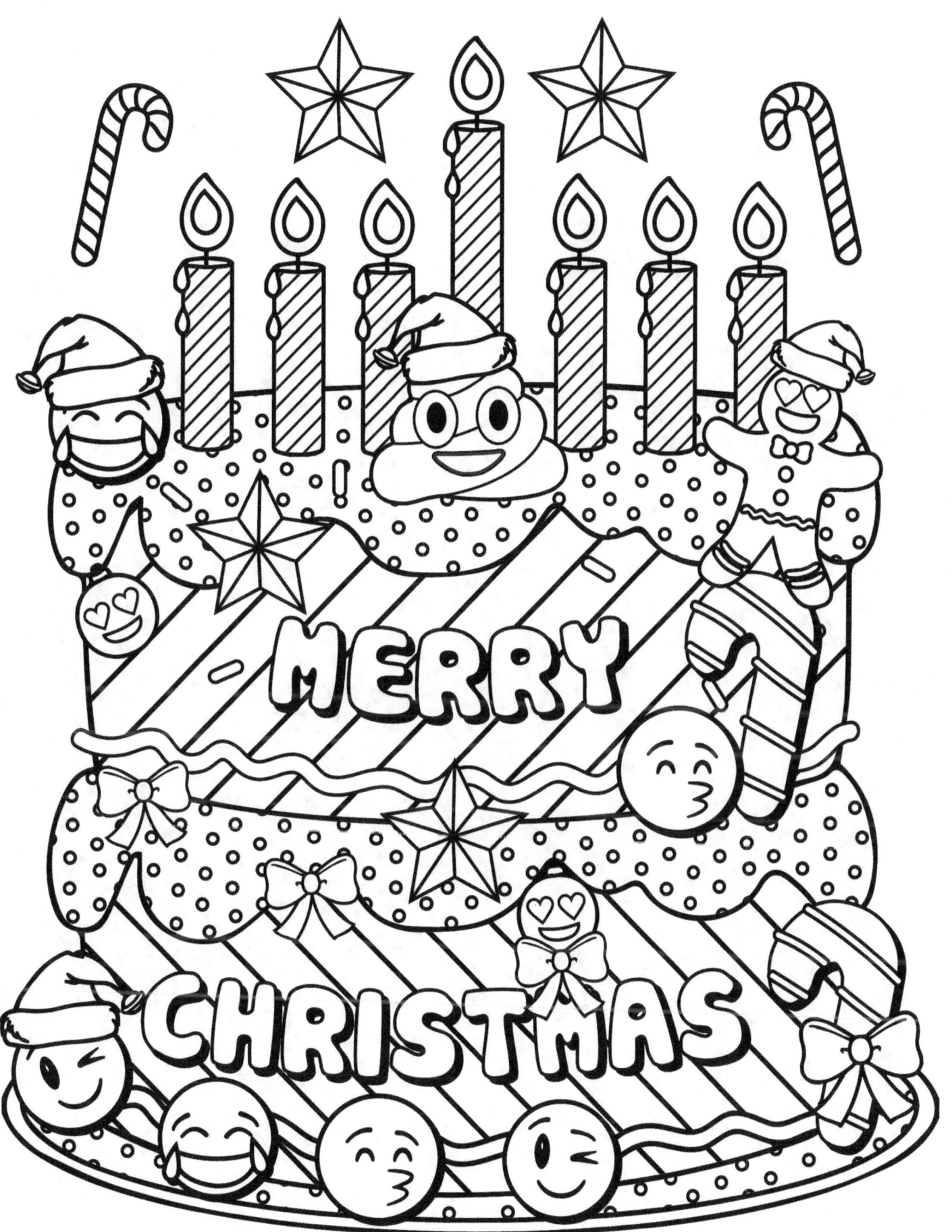

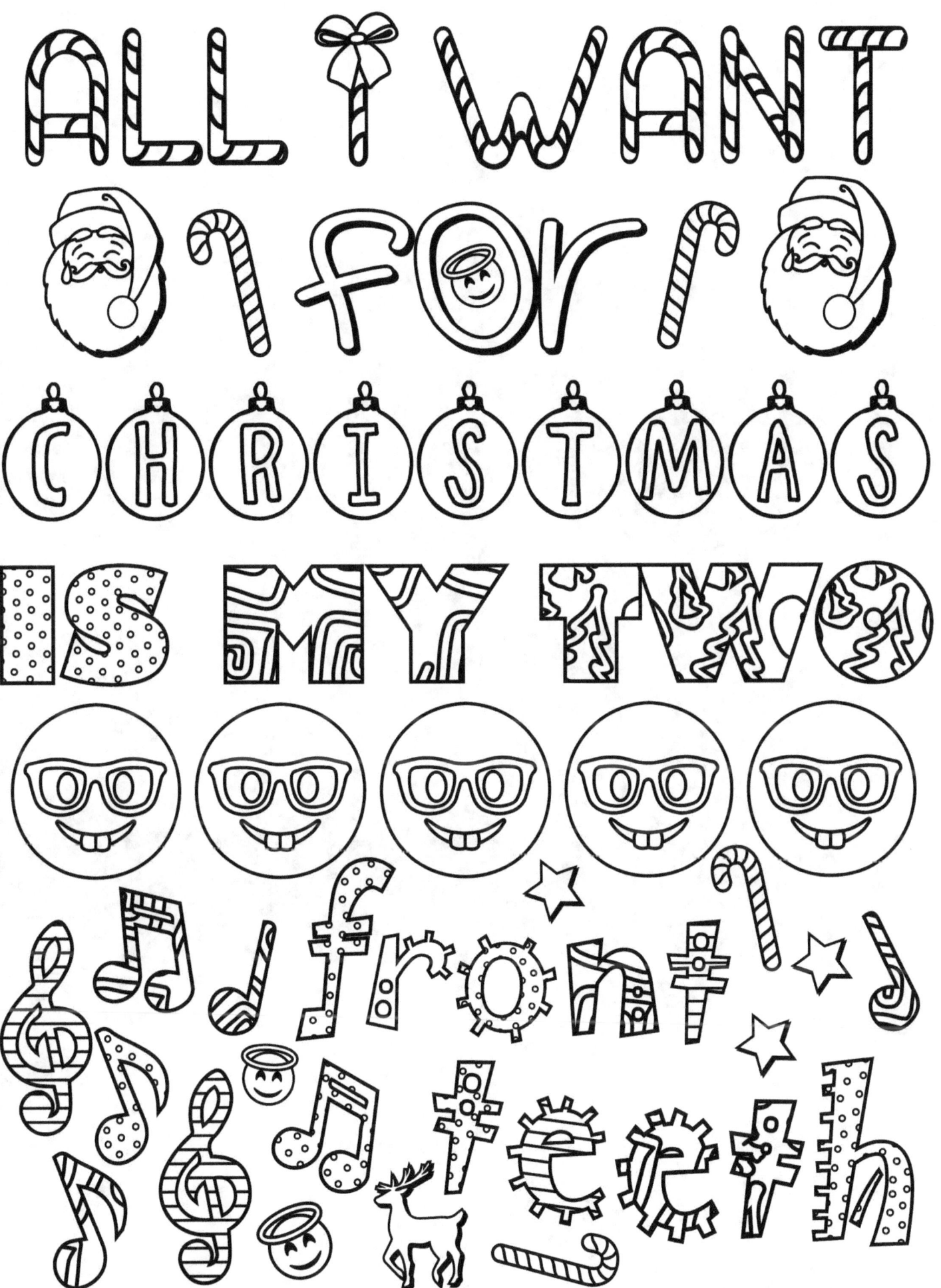

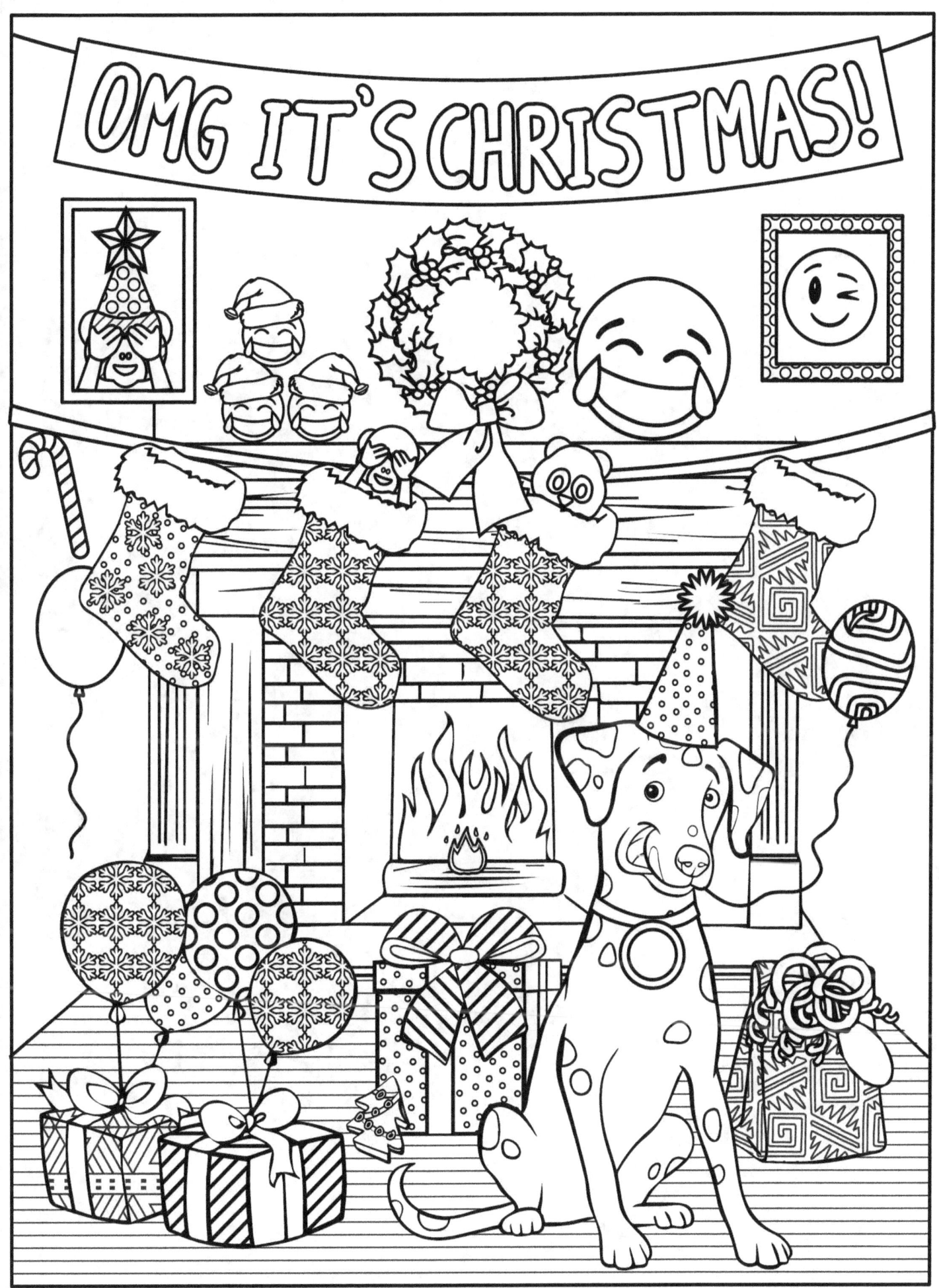

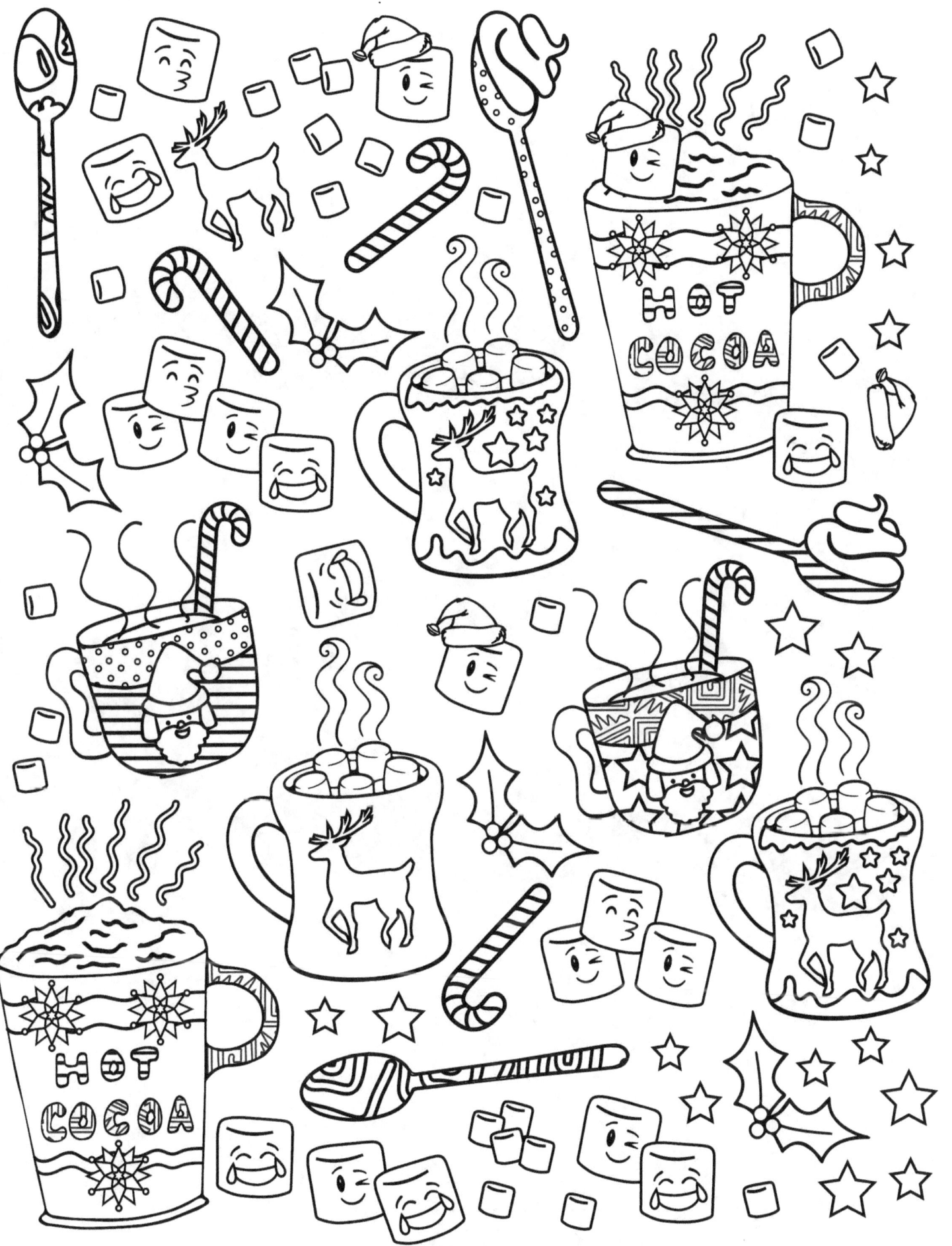

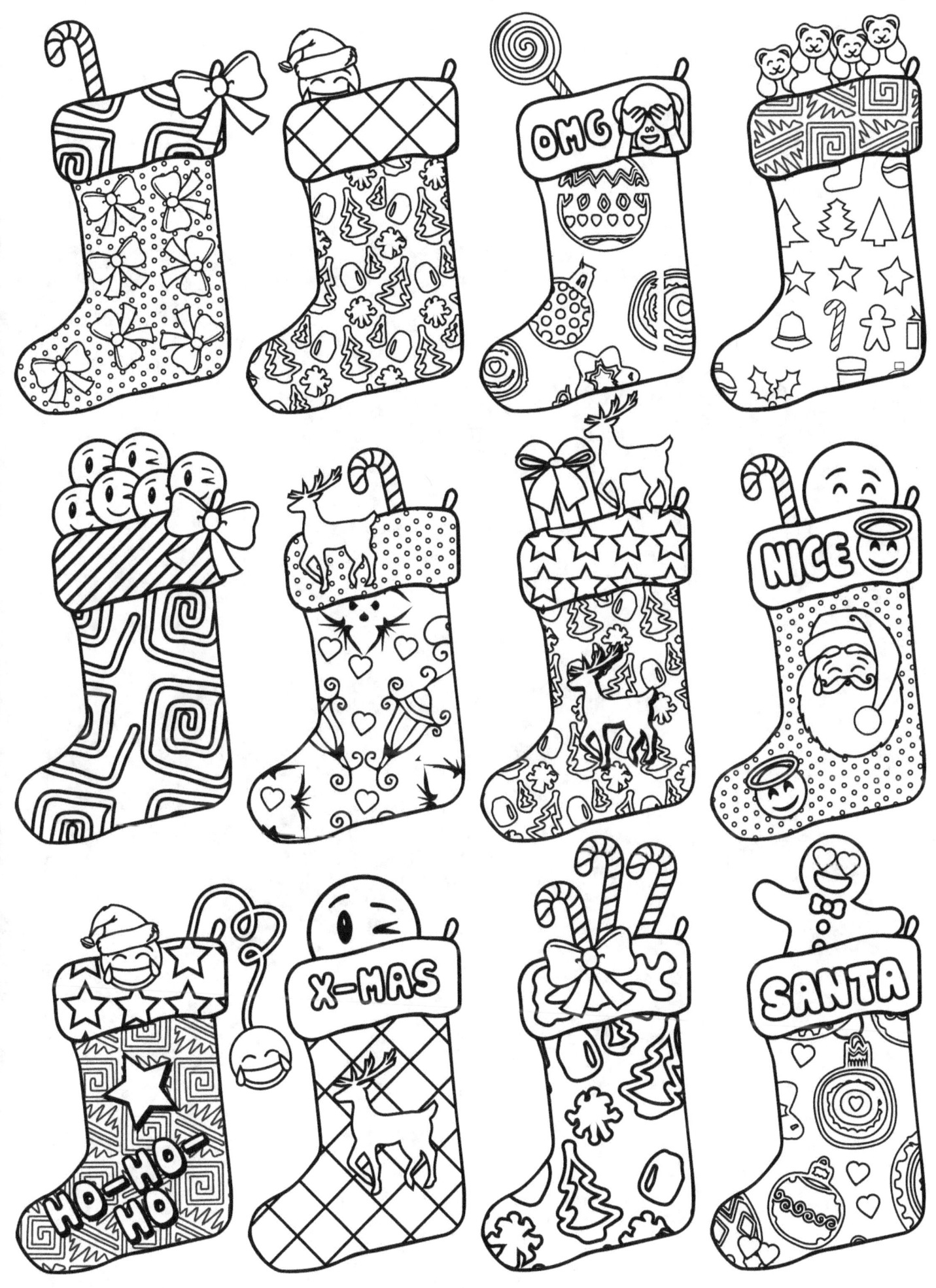

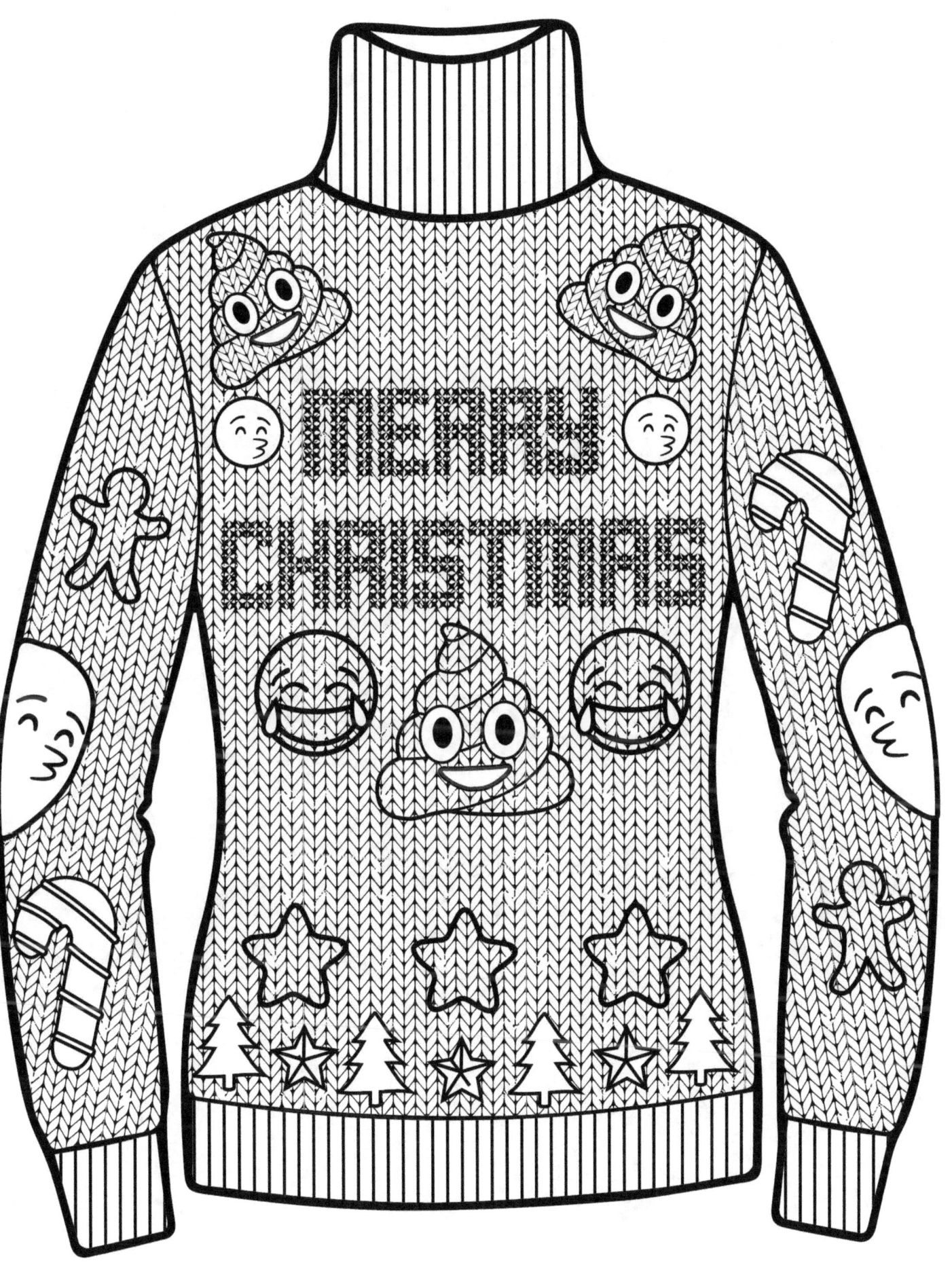

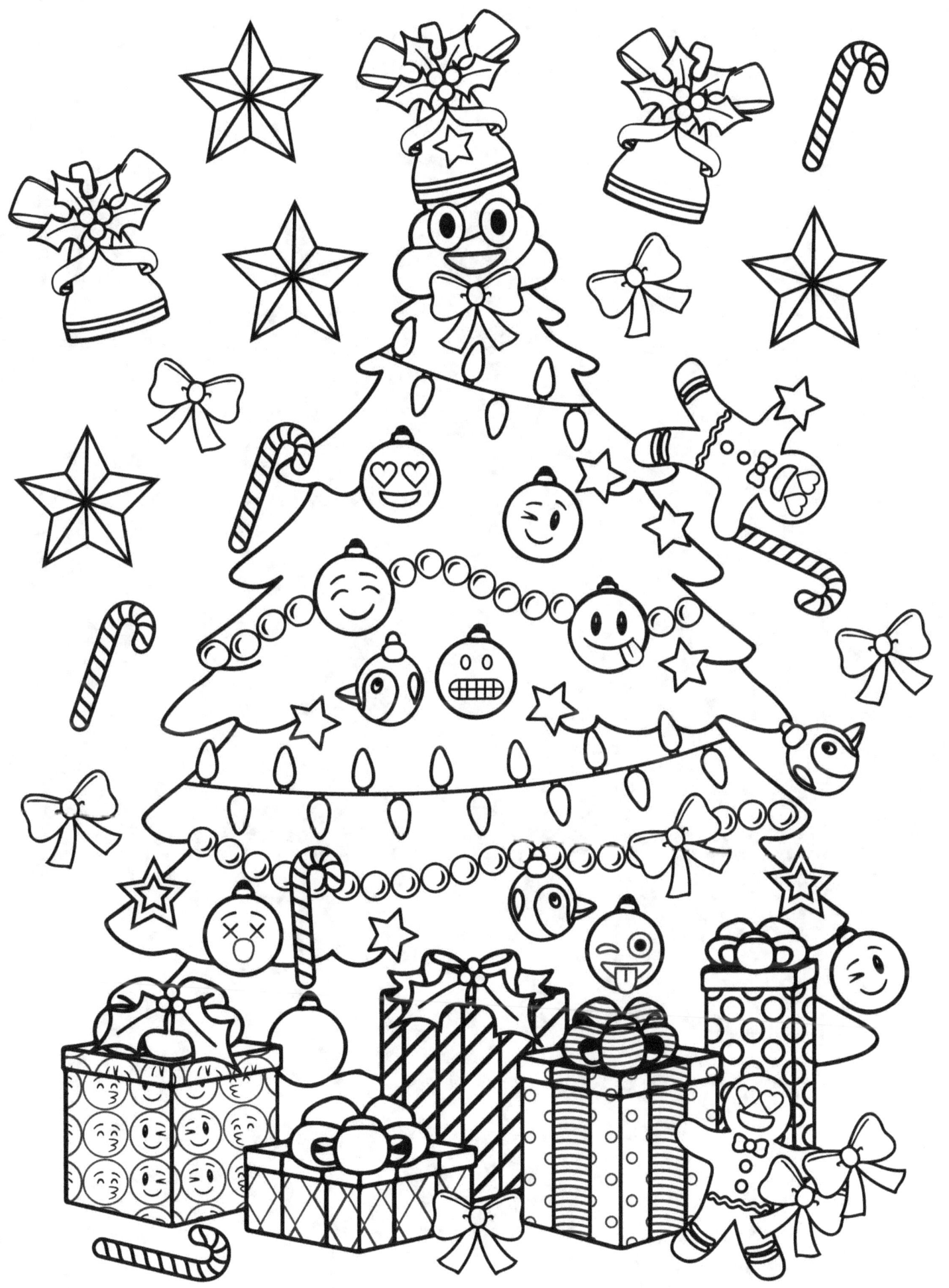

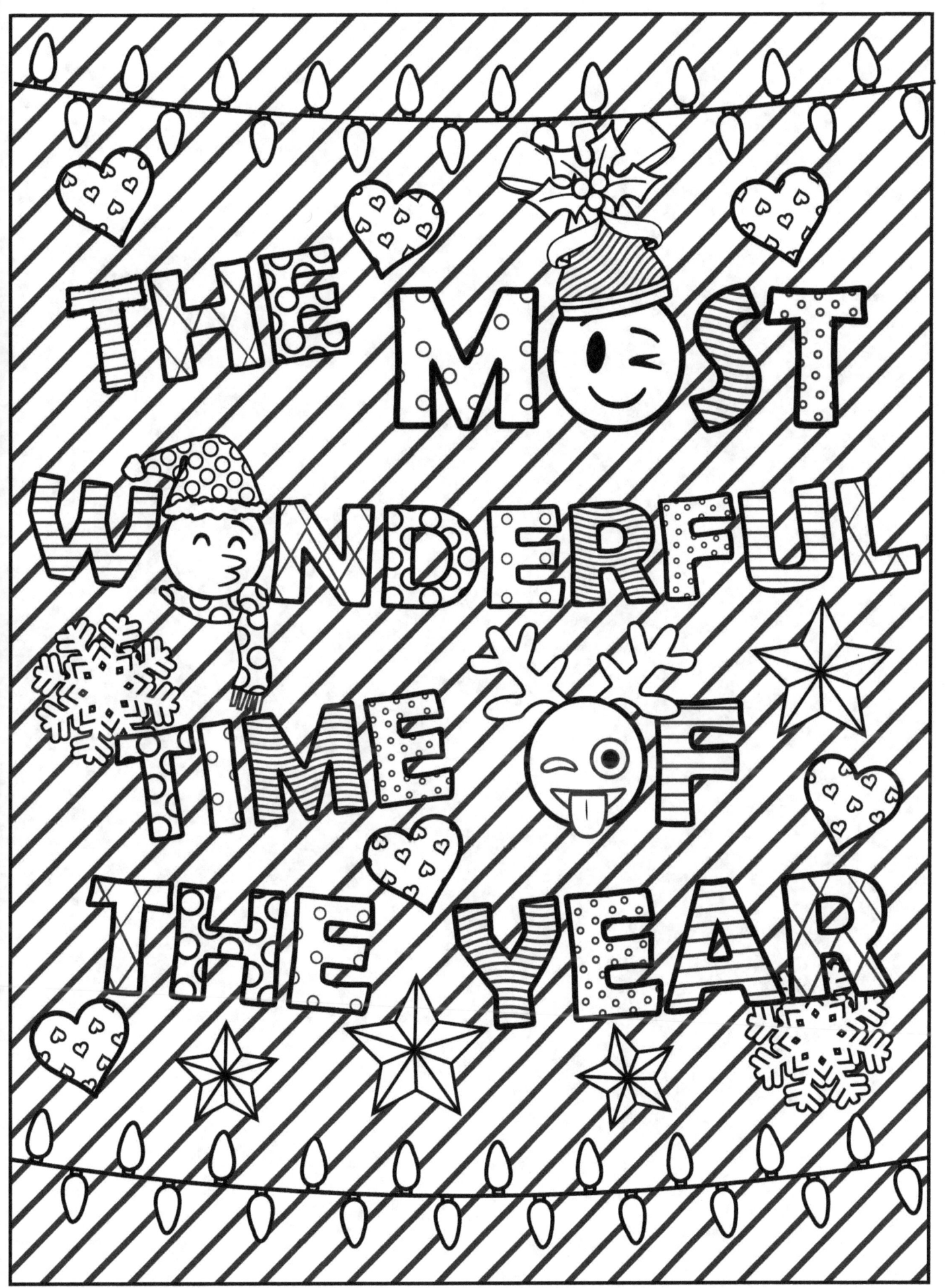

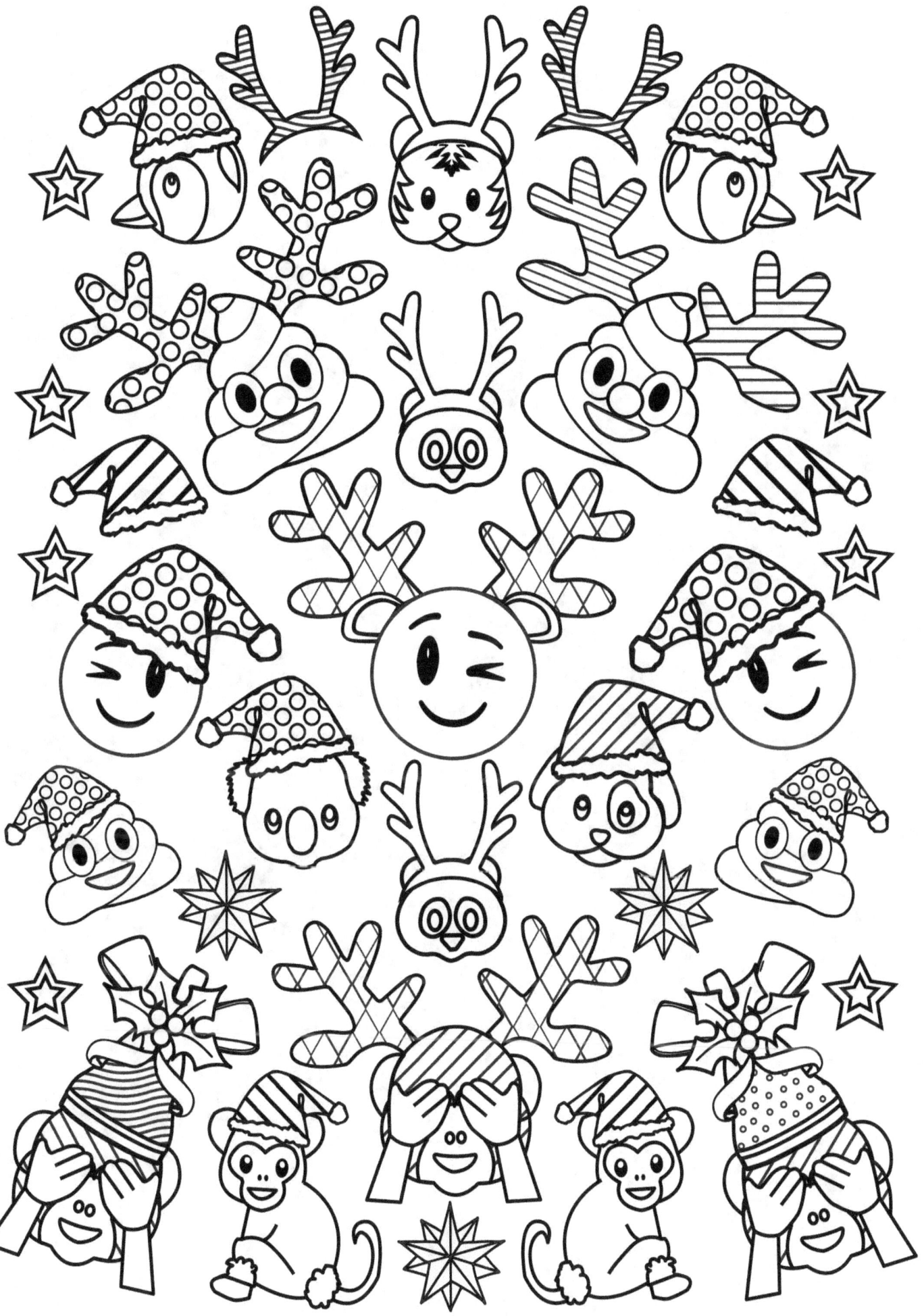

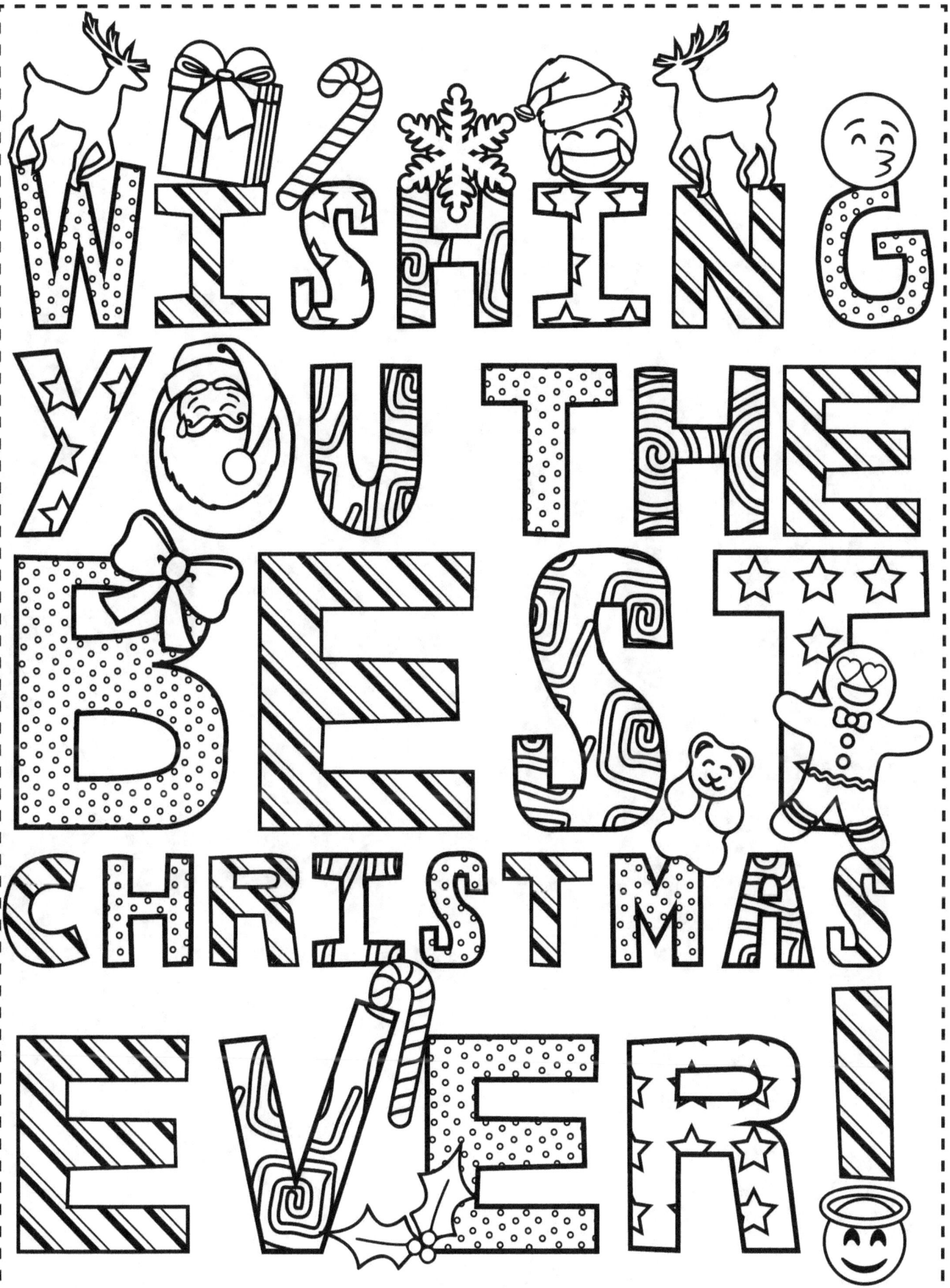

WISHING YOU THE BEST CHRISTMAS EVER!

cut with scissors (and give to someone special)

www.ingramcontent.com/pod-product-compliance
Lightning Source LLC
Chambersburg PA
CBHW081306180526

45170CB00007B/2589